AMERICAN PLACES
From Vision to Reality

The Empire State Building

by Meish Goldish

Consultants:
Carol A. Willis, Founder and Director
The Skyscraper Museum
New York, New York

Katie Uva, Andrew W. Mellon Foundation Predoctoral Fellow
Museum of the City of New York
New York, New York

BEARPORT
PUBLISHING

New York, New York

Credits

Cover, © Leonard Zhukovsky/Shutterstock; 2–3, © ThinAir/Shutterstock; 4, © AP Photo; 5, tinyurl.com/zppcfsz/Public Domain; 6L, Library of Congress; 6R, Library of Congress; 7L, © ID1974/Shutterstock; 7R, © Andrey Antipin/Shutterstock; 8, © John Arnold Images Ltd/Alamy Stock Photo; 9L, © Pictorial Press Ltd/Alamy Stock Photo; 9R, © Atomic/Alamy Stock Photo; 10, © Lebrecht Music and Arts Photo Library/Alamy Stock Photo; 11, © Image from the collection of The Skyscraper Museum; 12–13, tinyurl.com/zhlkvs6/Public Domain; 12T, © AP Photo; 14, © Image from the collection of The Skyscraper Museum; 15, © Image from the collection of The Skyscraper Museum; 16, © Everett Collection Inc/Alamy Stock Photo; 17L, tinyurl.com/h3epp2n/Public Domain; 17R, © Iurii Kachkovskyi/Shutterstock; 18, © Lewis W. Hine Glasshouse Images/Newscom; 19L, © Prisma Bildagentur AG/Alamy Stock Photo; 19R, © Bettmann/CORBIS; 20L, © Image from the collection of The Skyscraper Museum; 20R, © Image from the collection of The Skyscraper Museum; 21, © Image from the collection of The Skyscraper Museum; 22L, © AP Photo; 22R, © T Photography/Shutterstock; 23, © Matt Ragen/Shutterstock; 24, © AP Photo; 25L, © JASON SZENES UPI Photo Service/Newscom; 25R, © Ivan Marc/Shutterstock; 26T, © Pictorial Press Ltd/Alamy Stock Photo; 26B, © Pictorial Press Ltd/Alamy Stock Photo; 27, © Songquan Deng/Shutterstock; 28–29 (background), © robert_s/Shutterstock; 28, © Anton_Ivanov/Shutterstock; 29, © aurielaki/Alamy Stock Vector; 32, © Anton_Ivanov/Shutterstock.

Publisher: Kenn Goin
Editor: Jessica Rudolph
Creative Director: Spencer Brinker
Design: The Design Lab
Photo Researcher: Editorial Directions, Inc.

Library of Congress Cataloging-in-Publication Data

Names: Goldish, Meish, author.
Title: The Empire State Building / by Meish Goldish.
Description: New York, New York : Bearport Publishing, 2017. | Series: American places. From vision to reality | Includes bibliographical references and index.
Identifiers: LCCN 2016012274 (print) | LCCN 2016014023 (ebook) | ISBN 9781944102432 (library binding) | ISBN 9781944997120 (ebook)
Subjects: LCSH: Empire State Building (New York, N.Y.)—Juvenile literature.
 | New York (N.Y.)—Buildings, structures, etc.—Juvenile literature.
Classification: LCC F128.8.E46 G63 2017 (print) | LCC F128.8.E46 (ebook) | DDC 974.7—dc23
LC record available at http://lccn.loc.gov/2016012274

For more information, write to Bearport Publishing Company, Inc., 45 West 21st Street, Suite 3B, New York, New York 10010. Printed in the United States of America.

10 9 8 7 6 5 4 3 2 1

Contents

Scraping the Sky

In 1930, anyone walking down Fifth Avenue in New York City would have seen something amazing. At a construction site, groups of workers lifted giant **beams** across metal **columns** and connected them with **rivets**. It was a normal day on the job, except the men were hundreds of feet in the air! The workers were constructing the Empire State Building— the tallest **skyscraper** the world had ever seen.

The Empire State Building got its name from the nickname for New York State: The Empire State.

Working on the building was very dangerous. Men had to balance on the narrow beams, making sure they didn't lose their footing. One wrong move and a worker could **plummet** to the ground far below. As the building grew taller, workers rose toward the clouds to complete all 102 floors.

An Empire State Building worker sits on the edge of a beam.

In the early 1900s, nearly 200 skyscrapers were built in New York City. As more people and businesses crowded the city, the lack of space resulted in taller office buildings.

Making It Possible

The Empire State Building was the dream of John J. Raskob and Al Smith. The two men wanted to create a large office building for many of the city's growing businesses. Their goal was to construct an impressive structure that would stand out among all the other skyscrapers. One way to do this would be to make it taller than any other building. How could this be achieved?

John J. Raskob was a wealthy businessman.

Al Smith served as the governor of New York in the 1920s.

Before the late 1800s, most buildings were supported by wooden or stone walls. However, these materials weren't strong enough to support buildings much higher than ten stories. In 1855, a process was invented to make steel that was extremely strong and inexpensive. This steel could be used to make beams and columns that supported very tall buildings.

Elevator

Steel beams and columns

Another invention that made skyscrapers possible was the passenger elevator, developed in 1852. Elevators allow people to quickly and safely ride up to higher floors.

The Design

At the start of the huge project, Raskob and Smith found a site for the building—34th Street and Fifth Avenue, in the middle of the city. Then they hired **architects** and **engineers** to design it and plan the construction. In the final design, the building towered 1,250 feet (381 m) high. That was more than 200 feet (61 m) taller than the Chrysler Building, which, at the time, was the tallest building in the world.

Construction on the Chrysler Building, in New York City, was finished in 1930. It stands 77 stories and 1,046 feet (319 m) tall.

The Empire State Building's design included **setbacks**—places where the building gets narrower—and a mooring mast at the top. In the early 1930s, some people traveled long distances on **airships**, which are similar to blimps. Airships could dock at the mooring mast to let passengers on and off. Architects included the mast for another reason. It was a fairly inexpensive way to add extra height to the structure.

Mooring mast

Airship

R 101

G-FAAW

G   R 101

G

Setbacks

The Empire State Building has dozens of elevators. There are more of them at the lower floors than the top. The building was designed to be wider at the lower floors to make room for the elevators.

Tearing Down the Old

The spot at 34th Street and Fifth Avenue where Raskob and Smith chose to build their skyscraper was occupied by a famous hotel, the Waldorf-Astoria. The old structure had to be torn down before construction of the Empire State Building could start. On October 1, 1929, **demolition** began.

The Waldorf-Astoria Hotel

The demolition job took a few months. The work produced mountains of twisted metal and broken bricks. The **debris** from the Waldorf-Astoria Hotel was hauled away in trucks, then transferred to boats and dumped into the Atlantic Ocean about 20 miles (32 km) from shore.

The demolition of the Waldorf-Astoria

More than 16,000 truckloads of debris were dumped into the Atlantic Ocean!

Hard Times

While space was being cleared for New York's newest skyscraper, disaster struck. On October 29, 1929, the **stock market** crashed. Over the coming months and years, many businesses failed, and millions of workers lost their jobs. It was the start of a terrible time in the nation called the Great Depression.

A man tries to find a job during the Depression.

During the Depression, many out-of-work people could not afford food. They stood in line for meals that the government gave out for free.

The Stock Market Crash of 1929 did not stop Raskob and Smith, however. They decided to move ahead with their plans for the Empire State Building. The skyscraper stood as a symbol of hope for many during the hard times. The project offered work to thousands of people who were desperate for jobs—including construction workers and factory workers who provided steel, stone, wood, and glass for the building.

Starting at the Bottom

By January 1930, after land was cleared for the new skyscraper, hundreds of construction workers began building the **foundation**. Using dynamite and **steam shovels**, they blasted and dug out dirt and rocks in the ground until they hit solid **bedrock**.

Trucks carry loads of dirt and rocks out of the area cleared for the skyscraper's foundation.

Next, the structure of the skyscraper was laid out in a grid of big square bases. These bases, made of **concrete** and steel, would distribute the weight of the building above down to the bedrock. Upright steel columns placed on top of the bases looked like a forest of steel trees. These columns were the start of the building's **skeleton frame**.

Steel columns

Engineers figured that the skyscraper would weigh about 365,000 tons (331,122 metric tons)!

Teams at Work

After the upright columns were in place, workers used rivets to connect them to **horizontal** beams. Together, the steel columns and beams would complete the frame of the skyscraper. The men who did the riveting worked in teams of four, and each man had a different job.

Riveting teams completed four to five floors of the building's frame each week.

One type of worker, called the passer, began by heating a rivet in an oven. Then, using **tongs**, he tossed the rivet up into a bucket held by the catcher on the floor above. The catcher used tongs to place the red-hot rivet into holes in the two steel pieces being joined. The bucker-up used a bar to hold the rivet in place. Finally, the gunman pounded the soft rivet with a tool called an **air hammer**. The rivet then cooled and hardened, creating a solid connection between the two pieces of steel.

Rivets

A bucker-up (bottom right) holds a rivet in place as a gunman pounds it.

Young workers called water boys brought water to the thirsty construction crews.

"Don't Look Down!"

Workers risked their lives moving huge columns and beams into position and then riveting them together. Many of the workers, known as sky boys, were Mohawk Native Americans who had a lot of experience working on tall buildings. Walking along the narrow beams, the Mohawks advised other workers: "Don't look down! Look straight ahead at the end of the beam." This helped the men deal with their fear of heights.

Construction workers did their jobs high in the sky.

Sadly, five workers died in accidents while constructing the Empire State Building. One man was killed in a blast. The other men died when they fell from the skyscraper or were accidentally hit by heavy equipment.

Workers have a meal high up in the unfinished building.

A worker connects two cables.

Workers got their food from cafeterias constructed inside the building and then ate where they worked.

Finishing Up

Once the frame for each story of the skyscraper was completed, other builders got to work. Some attached blocks of stone to the frame to serve as the building's outer walls. Inside the structure, other workers built the floors, ceilings, and inner walls. Carpenters cut wood. Electricians installed wires. Plumbers laid water pipes. On the busiest days, more than 3,400 people worked on the Empire State Building.

This worker attaches wooden trim to an inner wall.

A worker plasters the ceiling of the fourth floor.

As the building grew, materials like heavy stone blocks had to be brought to higher and higher floors. Construction materials were lifted by hoists, which are similar to elevators. Each story had tracks that ran from the hoist to different parts of the floor. Workers loaded the materials onto flat cars and rolled them along the tracks to where they needed to go.

Pipes, wood, glass, and stone had to be delivered exactly on schedule. If materials arrived early, there was no place to store them. If they arrived late, workers couldn't finish their jobs on time.

Workers push a flat car along tracks to deliver heavy materials across a floor.

Opening Day

Workers completed the Empire State Building in a little over one year. On May 1, 1931, the world's tallest skyscraper officially opened. Raskob and Smith invited hundreds of special guests to the celebration. Even the president, Herbert Hoover, took part in the event. He pressed a button that turned on the building's lights.

Al Smith

A work of art on the lobby wall shows the Empire State Building.

Guests stand with Al Smith in the skyscraper's huge lobby on opening day.

More than 5,000 sightseers also filled the building on opening day. It cost adults 1 dollar and children 25 cents to visit the **observation deck** on the 86th floor. The sight from the deck was amazing. From so high up, viewers could see across the entire city.

A view of New York City from the 86th floor of the Empire State Building

Today, two observation decks are open to visitors— on the 86th and 102nd floors.

Repairs and Additions

Since 1931, the Empire State Building has seen many changes. In 1945, a pilot accidentally crashed a plane into the skyscraper, killing 14 people. The accident damaged three floors. However, the rest of the building was untouched and reopened just two days later. It took one year for the damaged floors to be repaired.

Investigators look at damage to the building after the plane crash in 1945.

In 1950, a television **antenna** and a **lightning rod** were added to the top of the building. When the building is struck by lightning, electricity passes safely down the rod, through the steel frame, and into the ground. The antenna and rod increased the skyscraper's record-breaking height to 1,454 feet (443 m).

Television antenna and lightning rod

Lightning strikes the Empire State Building about 100 times every year!

Airships were never able to dock on the skyscraper's mooring mast. High winds made landings too dangerous. By the late 1930s, airplane travel became more popular, and fewer people used airships.

A Building for All

Today, the Empire State Building serves as much more than just an office building. It's also a popular tourist destination. Every day, about 10,000 people visit the skyscraper. Many special events take place there as well. A race to the 86th floor is held yearly. The winner is usually able to run up the 1,576 stairs in only 10 minutes!

The Empire State Building has been featured in many movies. In the 1933 film *King Kong*, a giant ape climbs to the top of the mooring mast.

Tourists on the 86th floor observation deck

Throughout the year, the top of the building is lit in different colors to celebrate holidays and other important events. On the Fourth of July, its colors are red, white, and blue to match the American flag. Although the Empire State Building is no longer the world's tallest skyscraper, it remains one of the most well-known and beloved American **landmarks**.

The Empire State Building lit up to celebrate the Fourth of July

The Empire State Building was the world's tallest skyscraper until 1971. Today, the tallest building is the Burj Khalifa in western Asia. It stands 2,716.5 feet (828 m) tall.

The Empire State Building

It takes less than one minute to rise to the 80th floor by elevator. From there, a person can take another elevator to the 86th floor, and then another to the 102nd floor.

On a clear day, visitors at the observation deck on the 102nd floor can see 80 miles (129 km) away!

Number of Elevators: 73

Numbers of Visitors:
About 10,000 visitors a day; nearly 4 million every year

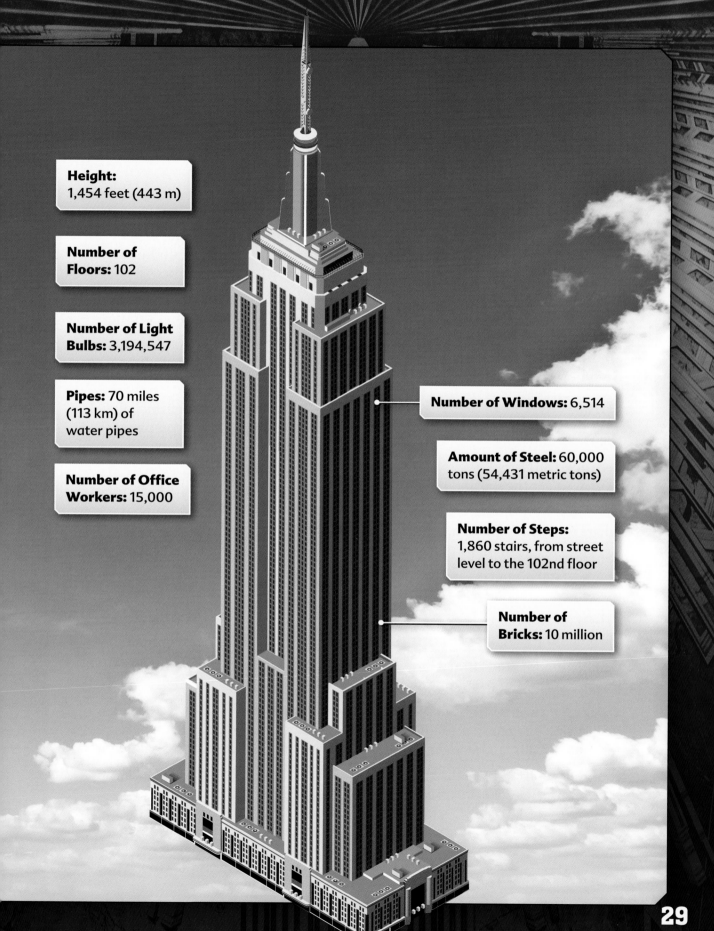

Height:
1,454 feet (443 m)

Number of Floors: 102

Number of Light Bulbs: 3,194,547

Pipes: 70 miles (113 km) of water pipes

Number of Office Workers: 15,000

Number of Windows: 6,514

Amount of Steel: 60,000 tons (54,431 metric tons)

Number of Steps: 1,860 stairs, from street level to the 102nd floor

Number of Bricks: 10 million

Glossary

air hammer (AIR HAM-ur) a powerful hand tool that uses compressed air to pound a metal piece such as a bolt

airships (AIR-ships) aircraft with engines and passenger compartments; they are filled with gas that is lighter than air to lift them off the ground

antenna (an-TEN-uh) a wire that receives radio and television signals

architects (AR-kih-tekts) people who design buildings

beams (BEEMZ) long, thick pieces of metal or wood used to support the floors of a building

bedrock (BED-rok) the solid layer of rock under the soil and loose rock

columns (KOL-uhmz) tall upright pillars that help support a building

concrete (kon-KREET) a mixture of sand, water, cement, and gravel used in construction

debris (duh-BREE) scattered pieces of something that has been destroyed

demolition (dem-uh-LISH-uhn) the knocking down of a building

engineers (en-juh-NIHRZ) people who design and construct buildings, machines, roads, and bridges

foundation (foun-DAY-shuhn) a solid base on which a structure is built

horizontal (hor-uh-ZON-tuhl) flat; level with the ground

landmarks (LAND-marks) buildings or places selected as important

lightning rod (LITE-ning ROD) a tool used to protect a building from damage by lightning strikes

observation deck (ob-zur-VAY-shuhn DEK) a place where things can be viewed from great distances

plummet (PLUHM-iht) drop suddenly

rivets (RIHV-its) strong, thick metal bolts that are used to fasten pieces of metal together

setbacks (SET-baks) sections of a building where walls are built back from the edge

skeleton frame (SKEL-ih-tuhn FRAYM) a basic structure over which something is built

skyscraper (SKYE-skray-pur) a very tall building

steam shovels (STEEM SHUHV-uhlz) machines used for digging large holes

stock market (STOK MAR-kiht) a place where stocks, or units of ownership in a company, are bought and sold

tongs (TAWNGZ) tools with connected arms used for picking things up

Bibliography

Holland, Gini. *The Empire State Building (Great Buildings).* Austin, TX: Raintree Steck-Vaughn (1998).

Reis, Ronald A. *The Empire State Building (Building America: Then and Now).* New York: Chelsea House (2009).

Read More

Bullard, Lisa. *The Empire State Building (Lightning Bolt Books).* Minneapolis, MN: Lerner (2010).

Hopkinson, Deborah, and James E. Ransome. *Sky Boys: How They Built the Empire State Building.* New York: Schwartz & Wade (2006).

Mann, Elizabeth. *Empire State Building: When New York Reached for the Skies (A Wonders of the World Book).* New York: Mikaya Press (2003).

Pascal, Janet B. *Where Is the Empire State Building?* New York: Grosset & Dunlap (2015).

Learn More Online

To learn more about the Empire State Building, visit:
www.bearportpublishing.com/AmericanPlaces

Index

About the Author

Meish Goldish has written more than 300 books for children. His book *City Firefighters* won a Teachers' Choice Award in 2015. He lives in Brooklyn, New York.